Crossing the Dead Line

by

Henry Clay Morrison

First Fruits Press
Wilmore, Kentucky
c2012

asburyseminary.edu
800.2ASBURY
204 North Lexington Avenue
Wilmore, Kentucky 40390

First Fruits
THE ACADEMIC OPEN PRESS OF ASBURY SEMINARY

ISBN: 9780984738793

Crossing the Dead Line, by H.C. Morrison.
First Fruits Press, © 2012
Pentecostal Publishing Company, © 1924

Digital version at http://place.asburyseminary.edu/firstfruitsheritagematerial/3/

Morrison, H. C. (Henry Clay) 1857-1942
    Crossing the dead line / by Henry Clay Morrison
    Wilmore, Ky. : First Fruits Press, c2012
    32 p. ; 21 cm.
    Reprint. Previously published: Crossing the dead line, or, The
    recrucifixion of the Lord Jesus Christ. Louisville, Ky. : Pentecostal Pub.
    Co., c1924.
    9780984738793 (pbk.)
    1. Theology, Doctrinal. I. Title.
    BT78 .M84 2012

Cover design by Haley Hill

asburyseminary.edu
800.2ASBURY
204 North Lexington Avenue
Wilmore, Kentucky 40390

First Fruits
THE ACADEMIC OPEN PRESS OF ASBURY SEMINARY

Crossing the Dead Line

OR

The Recrucifixion of the Lord Jesus Christ

BY

REV. H. C. MORRISON, D.D.

Author of "The Baptism with the Holy Ghost," "Dr Star
and the White Temple," "Thoughts for the Thought-
ful," "Sermons for the Times," "World Tour
of Evangelism," "The Two Lawyers," "The
Second Coming of Christ," and
other volumes.

PENTECOSTAL PUBLISHING COMPANY,
Louisville, Ky.

DEDICATION.

This booklet is affectionately dedicated to the young ministers of Methodism North and South, East and West, with the prayer that those who read its pages may guard themselves with great care against any deviation from the saving truths of the Holy Scriptures and a personal trust for full salvation in the merits of our blessed Lord and Redeemer.

PREFACE.

The matter contained in this booklet has been largely delivered in some addresses from the Chapel platform of Asbury College. Some of this matter has been used in several sermons at camp meetings and other religious gatherings. A good many friends, as well as myself, feel that the contents of this booklet may be of special value at this time.

I grieve over the loss of any man's soul. I believe those men, college professors, preachers, students and all men and women who are departing from the faith, who are speaking lightly of the written Word of God, and the Son of God, have gone into a fearful apostasy. I have no faith in the faith of those whose faith does not embrace the Lord Jesus as God manifest in the flesh and dying on the Cross for the free and full redemption of all those who come to God by Him. Let those who read the contents of this booklet pass it on to others. If the blessing of God may attend it and it may be used to prevent the apostasy of some precious soul, I shall be thankful.

CROSSING THE DEADLINE,

OR

THE RECRUCIFIXION OF THE LORD JESUS CHRIST.

Text: "But there were false prophets
also among the people, even as
there shall be false teachers among
you, who privily shall bring in
damnable heresies, even denying
the Lord that bought them, and
bring upon themselves swift destruction. And many shall follow
their pernicious ways; by reason of
whom the way of truth shall be
evil spoken of. And through covetousness shall they with feigned
words make merchandise of you;
whose judgment now of a long time
lingereth not, and their damnation
slumbereth not."—II. Peter 2:1-3.

St. Peter was not only an apostle; he
was also a prophet. In his Second
Epistle, he foretells conditions which
actually exist in the world today with
an accuracy which places upon his writings the positive stamp of divine inspiration.

In the first chapter of this same Epistle, he calls attention to the "sure word of prophecy" and exhorts us to take heed to the same "as to a light that shineth in a dark place." He then gives us assurance of the trustworthiness of prophecy, saying, "For the prophecy came not in old time by the will of man, but holy men of God spake as they were moved by the Holy Ghost." Then he calls attention in the words of the text to the fact that as there were false prophets in the past, there shall be false teachers among you; that is, in the church of New Testament times. In the text and some verses connected with the text, he foretells conditions that exist in the church today in many countries as accurately as if his Epistle had been written last week instead of almost two thousand years ago.

The only rational way in which we can account for Peter's accurate description of the widespread skepticism within the church at the present time is to admit that the Holy Spirit who foresaw these conditions inspired Peter to write what we find here in our text and the verses connected with the text. I want you to go with me into an examination of these Scriptures: "There shall be false teachers among you who privily shall bring in damnable heresies." I think it is a fact which will be admitted by all well informed persons that we have many teachers and preachers in our midst today who are denying the inspiration of much of the Holy Scriptures contained in Old Testament and New. These false teachers tell us that Moses did not write the Pentateuch. They ignore the fact that our Lord Jesus often quoted from Moses. On one occasion, He said, "For had ye believed Moses, ye would have believed me: for he wrote of me. But if ye believe not his writings, how shall ye believe my words?"   It will be found that those teachers who would discount the writings of Moses will also discount the words of Jesus.   These false teachers do not hesitate to deny the Mosaic account of the Flood, although Jesus places His endorsement upon that account.   The same is true with reference to the Bible account of Jonah's peculiar experience.   Jesus fully endorses this Bible record, but the false teachers deny with ridicule the Bible story of Jonah notwithstanding   Christ's   statement with reference to the same.

The   contradiction   of   these   false teachers of the writings of Moses, the prophets, the teachings of Christ and the writings of the Apostles, are so frequent, emphatic, extensive and irreverent that it is impossible to retain our faith in the inspiration of the Bible, in the Virgin Birth and Atonement made by our Lord Jesus and at the same time accept the contradiction of these teachers and preachers who claim to be sent of God and to have a reliable message of helpfulness to mankind. Without doubt these men in high places and low who are making constant assaults upon the inspiration of the Bible are the false teachers spoken of by the Apostle Peter in our text. He speaks of them in the plainest terms. He says, "They will bring in damnable heresies." His words are positive. His meaning is plain. Their heresies can but lead to the loss of saving faith in our Lord Jesus, the casting away of the truth, the destruction of all spiritual life in the church, the undermining of all the high moral sentiment that arises out of Christian faith, and the ultimate destruction of countless human souls.

The destructive criticism of the Holy Scriptures which has been rampant in

Germany for the past half century, has wrought spiritual and moral ruin in that country. It has had time to produce its legitimate fruit and the fearful conditions existing in that country and among those great and capable people at the present time reveal what must inevitably occur when the Word of God is discarded, the Son of God is rejected, and the Holy Spirit is grieved away. There are no greater people physically, mentally and industrially than the German people. They are one of the most aggressive and productive peoples in the world; but for the false teachers in their universities and pulpits, they would be one of the most devout and spiritual people in the world today. The conditions which brought on the World War could not have existed, the savagery and ruin wrought by these otherwise great people, that has brought distress and confusion to the nations of the earth and laid a staggering burden upon the shoulders of the present generation and that which is to come, could never have come into our world but for the false teachers in universities and pulpits who brought in the "damnable heresies" that have turned loose fire, and sword and plague, confusion and death in the earth.

This same blight of heretical teaching is quenching the spiritual fires in England, has swept over Canada and is becoming a widespread plague and curse in these United States.

It is a notable fact that these false teachers who deny the inspiration of much of the Bible, have been at no pains to point out those portions of the Scriptures that they believe to be inspired. They boldly declare in direct contradiction to the Word of God that there has been no fall of the race, that there is no such thing as inherited depravity;

hence, no need of a New Birth or cleansing away of sin and as a natural consequence no need of an atonement; therefore, no necessity for the tragedy of the cross which they insist might have been avoided. Thus, they would rob us of the entire meaning of all the ancient sacrifices of the Israelitish people. They would strip the prophecies of all their deep and wonderful significance, tear out from the Bible all account of the miracles performed by our Lord, with ruthless hands chop down the cross and cut the heart out of the Gospel, fling aside the teachings of the apostles, tear up the hymn books, raze the foundations of the church and plunge the world into midnight darkness and blasphemous unbelief.

We must not pass without notice this word, 'PRIVILY.' It is a most significant and interesting fact that these false teachers bring in their heresies in the very way indicated by St. Peter. How different the methods of the disciples of doubt, the apostles of unbelief, in their propaganda from the methods of John Wesley, General Booth, Charles Finney and Dwight L. Moody. These great evangelical teachers in their proclamation of the Gospel always sought the greatest possible publicity. They strove to get to the multitudes of people with the glad, good news of a Redeemer mighty to save to the uttermost.

The destructive critics and this whole brood of false teachers use shrewd and deceptive methods. They do not come bravely into the open with their declarations; they dare not call a public convention of their cult, openly declare to the public that the Bible is a forgery, that Jesus Christ is not divine, that the Christian Church is founded upon falsehood. They are not set on fire with a holy enthusiasm that leads them to give up their salaries, surrender their chairs in Christian schools, go out into the streets and highways like the true disciples of a new-found truth, build their own churches and schools, support themselves, suffer privation and set on foot an active propaganda for the rescue of the perishing, the salvation of souls and the uplift of the race. Such procedure is entirely foreign to them, but they are careful to slip their poison into the literature of the Church, and into the classrooms of the schools. It is their delight to get before a summer school of young preachers and dilute the pure faith of the ministry with their false philosophies. They undertake and largely succeed in "privily" drawing away young men, in theological schools and other institutions from the faith of the fathers and sending them out to preach—what! If the Ten Commandments were written by ancient pagans who knew nothing of God they are not inspired and ought not to be preached as a divine revelation. If the prophets of old knew nothing of the coming Messiah, what they have written certainly has no place in the pulpit. If Jesus was not of Virgin Birth, therefore not a divine being and made no atonement for sin on the Cross, then of course He ought not to be offered to the people as a Saviour. All of this heresy is the stock in trade of quite an army of false teachers in our country today who are eating the bread of the Church while they "privily" pour their false teachings through the channels of the church and lead the people away from the faith in Christ that alone can save the souls of men. Like thieves in the night they are stealing away the beautiful and priceless jewels of the Gospel which is the power of God unto salvation to every one that believeth.

These false teachers, you may be sure, are not kindling revival fire. They are not rescuing the perishing. They are not bringing back the fallen, the drunkard, the harlot, the outcast and the infidel from the far country of sin to a saving faith in our Lord Jesus. On the other hand, they are sowing broadcast by sly and shrewd methods the seeds of the most dangerous, insinuating and deceptive skepticism that has ever been invented and propagated by the enemies of our Lord Jesus and His Church.

The great fundamental truths of the Bible, the truths held tenaciously by the devoted followers of Christ, the foundation principles of our holy Christianity, for which saints and martyrs have suffered through the ages and which like torches of sacred fire have illuminated the dark places of the earth and have kindled powerful revivals of religion throughout the nation, have become subjects for the amusement and ridicule of these false teachers. They actually rejoice when they can break up the faith of the young people in their congregations in the Church or their classes in the schools.

St. Peter calls our attention to the fact that in their blindness and the extravagance and boldness of their infidelity, they will, "even deny the Lord that bought them." This is a fearful climax of infidelity. This is a crucifixion of the Son of God afresh. They thus put our Lord Jesus to an open shame before the world.

Some months ago there was sent broadcast through this country a pamphlet containing a sermon preached by one of these false teachers. The sermon was preached in one of the large and influential churches of one of our great cities. In this sermon, this high priest of the destructive critic school tells us that much of the Old Testament is not inspired, he flatly denies the Virgin Birth of our Lord Jesus, he denies the apostolic account of the miracles wrought by our Lord during His earthly ministry. He also denies the blood atonement made upon the cross. He produces no proof to substantiate these denials. There is no such proof. He simply sets up his unbelief against the inspired statement of prophets, Christ and the apostles. Is not this denying the Lord that bought him? What more could an outspoken infidel do? Of course there is nothing new in these denials. Tom Paine, Robert Ingersoll and the blatant and profane infidels of the past have all denied the Virgin Birth of Jesus, the miracles, the whole scheme of human redemption brought to its climax in the death of our Lord upon the cross. This licensed skeptic, who has had laid upon him the hands of the Church in consecration simply repeats the unbelief of the old Jews who crucified our Lord and of the skeptics that have blasted and destroyed the souls of men throughout the history of the Church. One is appalled to think of a man claiming to be a God-sent minister standing in the sacred desk and "DENYING THE LORD WHO BOUGHT HIM." Does not such a man belong to that class of false teachers spoken of by the Apostle Peter? Can there be any hope for the salvation of one who would rob Jesus of His deity and do away with the atonement made by Him when He took our sins in His own body on the tree of the cross and by the grace of God tasted death for every man?

If such a man has ever been regenerated, is he not described by the inspired writer in the Epistle to the Hebrews, "For it is impossible for those who were once enlightened, and have tasted of the heavenly gift, and were made partakers of the Holy Ghost, and have tasted the good word of God, and the powers of the world to come, if they shall fall away, to renew them again unto repentance; seeing they crucify to themselves the Son of God afresh, and put him to an open shame?" Let it be remembered here that the inspired Apostle does not refer to the lapses, stumblings, and backslidings of the Christian. Backsliders can be reclaimed. Many prodigals have wandered far from the Father's house and come back to be received with joy. The Apostle undoubtedly is calling attention here to those who listened to the Judaizing teachers, who infested the Church in the days of the Apostle Paul and strove to seduce those who had been converted to Christ to give up the faith in Christ and to turn back to the ceremonial law and thereby deny the deity and the atonement made by Jesus. These are the people who could not be renewed to repentance, who had crossed the deadline because, having repudiated and re-crucified Jesus by their denial, there was for them no possibility of salvation. What was true then is true today. The saddest and most startling feature of this whole subject of Modernism is that it is leading multitudes of people to repudiate their faith, to turn entirely away from the atonement made by our Lord and thus to seal their doom and make impossible an evangelical repentance and a saving faith.

The text teaches us further that as a result of these false teachers "many shall follow their pernicious ways by reason of whom the way of truth shall be evil spoken of." This prophecy is being fulfilled before our very eyes. Many of these false teachers are men of education, of polished manners, of a large degree of personal magnetism. They are skillful at covering up the logical outcome of their teaching. They work "privily." They deceive the people and many are following their pernicious ways. Great congregations are being captured and led blindly into the ditch of a fatal skepticism and by reason of this tremendous drift from the anchorage of truth in the church "the way of truth shall be evil spoken of." The newspapers, the magazines, the fiction writers seize upon this current of unbelief, hold up the sacred truths of the Bible to ridicule and great masses of sinners on the outside of the Church are led to speak evil of Christ, of His Bride, the Church, His saving power and thus the trickling rills of false teaching in school, pulpit and printed page, and conversation, makes a great river of skepticism rising higher and higher and flooding the land with an unbelief that obliterates reverence and the fear of God from the hearts of the multitude. Crime increases as unbelief spreads and finally unregenerated and godless rulers fall out among themselves, war breaks out, there is blood and fire on every hand and when the men who have sown the seed begin to reap the harvest, they blaspheme God and say, "If there was a merciful God in the universe He would not permit such havoc among men."

The third verse of this remarkable chapter from which we take our text, is very suggestive and accurately describes conditions now existing: "And through covetousness shall they with feigned words make merchandise of you." The destructive critics who have cast aside the Gospel and are doing nothing for the conversion of the souls of men and the perfecting of the saints are notably money-hungry. They are always and everywhere insisting on collections of money. The fact is, having given up the Holy Scriptures, they are ready to sell the Lord Jesus for some millions of dollars, for instead of trusting in His Gospel and the atoning merit of His blood to save the world, they have gotten the conceited and false notion that they can save the world with money, but they must become skillful in the use of "feigned words." They are experts in stirring the people to greater efforts in money-gathering with a pretense of piety and a mechanical use of Scripture terms which are thoroughly disgusting to those who know the truth and love the Lord as they go about the earth gathering in millions for which they gladly sell our Lord Jesus. Meanwhile they seek to elevate false teachers into places of trust, into educational institutions and office. They search diligently for those who are tinctured with modernism for the mission fields. They put obstructions in the way of the consecrated, Spirit-filled, God-called missionaries, and in many ways with "feigned words" they deceive the people, get their money and hinder the spread of a pure and powerful Gospel.

One stands amazed as he looks upon these conditions and sees how rapidly the propaganda of skepticism has made headway in these United Stats, and how bold and aggressive the false teachers have become in their assault upon the very foundations of our holy religion. Peter assures us that their judgment will come. He very clearly indicates that their boasted scholarship and their high ecclesiastical positions will by no means protect them from the wrath of God, but that bye and bye Judgment will break forth upon those who have darkened counsel, poisoned the very springs of spiritual life and brought down destruction upon the innocent and unsuspecting multitudes. "If," says the Apostle, "God spared not the angels that sinned, but cast them down to hell and delivered them into chains of darkness to be reserved unto judgment." This is a most suggestive warning to the cultured, boastful, pampered, irreverent skeptic in church school and pulpit who are privily attacking the Holy Scriptures, who are tearing to tatters the Word of God, who are insinuating that our Lord Jesus was of sinful birth and that His death on the cross was entirely unnecessary, that in His suffering there was no atonement. Their day of judgment will come. These unfortunate and irreverent men and the host of silly women who are being deceived and running away from Jesus in their enthusiasm and devotion to attractive and shrewd deceivers must stand before the Throne of the Christ they are re-crucifying and putting to an open shame.

I have felt constrained for months to lift up my voice in earnest protest and faithful warning to the people of my times who are being deceived. who are being led away from the Christ, who are being made to feel that it is a mark both of intelligence and of piety to doubt, to treat with irreverence the Word of God, to trample under foot the blood of the everlasting covenant as an unholy thing. I would voice again the earnest warnings and exhortations of the inspired Apostle as he describes the false teachers who privily and with covetous spirits and feigned words lead the people away from the only possible source of salvation. The Holy Spirit through the pen of Peter draws an accurate and fearful picture of these false teachers in the following words:

"These are wells without water, clouds that are carried with a tempest; to whom the mist of darkness is reserved forever. For when they speak great swelling words of vanity, they allure through the lusts of the flesh, through much wantonness, those that were clean escaped from them who live in error. While they promise them liberty, they themselves are the servants of corruption: for of whom a man is overcome, of the same is he brought in bondage."—II. Peter 2:17, 18, and 19.

Let it be remembered by those who are disposed to take liberties with the Word of God, to question its divine authority, and to speak lightly of the Christ of prophecy and the gospels, that there is a *dead line*. "Mercy knows the appointed bounds and turns to vengeance there."

The re-crucifixion of Jesus is no ordinary sin. It is the sin of those who once knew him as Lord and Savior, who have "tasted the heavenly gift" of pardon, who have known the witness of the Holy Ghost; the Word of God has been precious to them, and they felt the thrill of "the powers of the world to come." But they have fallen away; they have listened to the voice of the deceiver. In some summer schools for young preachers, or Sabbath school teachers, they have been drawn away from the Christ they once knew and trusted in for salvation. They have repudiated him; they have been persuaded that he was a mere man, not of miraculous virgin birth, not the Son of God in any sense in which other men may not be; and they have gone so far as to reject the atonement made by Christ, and have cast his atoning mercy entirely away from them. They have crucified the Son of God afresh, have given God the lie, and are left without a Savior, and their doom is sealed.

John tells us, "He that believeth on the Son of God hath the witness in himself; he that believeth not God hath made him a liar, because he believeth not the record that God gave of his Son." It is here made to appear that it is a serious matter to doubt or deny the sonship and godhead of Jesus Christ. "He that hath the Son hath life; and he that hath not the Son of God hath not life."

To have Christ and the life he bestows is to believe the record God has given of him in Old Testament and New. It is to believe that he is the only begotten of the Father, full of grace and truth. It is to believe in the atonement he made for us on the cross and thus believing in him, to believe on him for personal salvation. It means to trust in him who died for us, who paid our debt in his vicarious sufferings for our sins in our stead.

To deny the record that God has given of his Son is to deny the deity of his Son and the blood atonement he has made for us; it is to re-crucify Christ; it is to cross the deadline and go out into a region of doubt and darkness, and death beyond, and the reach of any possibility of salvation.

St. Paul pictures the situation of such a soul in most solemn words, saying, "He that despised Moses' law died without mercy under two or three witnesses. Of how much sorer punishment, suppose ye, shall he be thought worthy, who hath trodden under foot the Son of God, and hath counted the blood of the covenant, wherewith he was sanctified, an unholy thing, and hath done despite unto the Spirit of grace." Heb. 10:28, 29. What a fearful hour when these poor deluded men, these deceivers of the people, shall "fall into the hands of the living God." In the day of judgment I would rather be the ancient Jews who spat upon our Lord on the day of his crucifixion, than to be the modern preacher or college professor who denies the deity of our Lord and discounts the virtue of the blood he shed and the life he poured out upon the cross for our sins.

Life is short; soon those pampered preachers, who tickle the ears of their wealthy and godless congregations, will fall in death; their blasphemous lips will be forever silent, and they will go up to stand before the Christ whose blood they have counted an unholy thing.

www.ingramcontent.com/pod-product-compliance
Lightning Source LLC
Chambersburg PA
CBHW030313030426
42337CB00012B/693